better together*

* This book is best read together, grownup and kid.

 **akidsco.com**

a kids
book
about

a kids book about

mental health

by Dr. Katie Lingras

A Kids Co.
Editor Emma Wolf
Designer Rick DeLucco
Creative Director Rick DeLucco
Studio Manager Kenya Feldes
Sales Director Melanie Wilkins
Head of Books Jennifer Goldstein
CEO and Founder Jelani Memory

DK
Delhi Technical Team Bimlesh Tiwary Pushpak Tyagi, Rakesh Kumar
Senior Production Editor Jennifer Murray
Senior Production Controller Louise Minihane
Senior Acquisitions Editor Katy Flint
Acquisitions Project Editor Sara Forster
Managing Art Editor Vicky Short
Managing Director, Licensing Mark Searle

First American edition, 2025
Published in the United States by DK Publishing, 1745 Broadway, 20th Floor,
New York, NY 10019

First published in Great Britain in 2025 by
Dorling Kindersley Limited, 20 Vauxhall Bridge Road, London SW1V 2SA
A Penguin Random House Company

The authorised representative in the EEA is
Dorling Kindersley Verlag GmbH. Arnulfstr. 124, 80636 Munich, Germany

A catalog record for this book is available from the Library of Congress.
A CIP catalogue record for this book is available from the British Library.
ISBN: 978-0-2417-4347-8

DK books are available at special discounts when purchased in bulk for sales
promotions, premiums, fund-raising, or education use. For details, contact:
DK Publishing Special Markets, 1745 Broadway, 20th Floor, New York, NY 10019
SpecialSales@dk.com

Printed and bound in China
www.dk.com
akidsco.com

MIX
Paper | Supporting
responsible forestry
FSC™ C018179

This book was made with Forest
Stewardship Council™ certified
paper – one small step in DK's
commitment to a sustainable future.
Learn more at www.dk.com/uk/
information/sustainability

To my nieces and nephews, Alexander, Kira, Teresa, Oliver, Will, Jacob, Ben, and Danny— I pictured reading this book with each of you as I wrote it!

To all the children and families I have worked with—you taught me as much as I taught you!

To the grownups—including my own parents—who muddled through these conversations without the benefit of resources (like this one) available today.

To my MACMH-IEC, UMN "frolleagues", spouse, and chosen family—thank you for helping me think through this book and for supporting my mental health on a regular basis!

Intro
for grownups

Did you know that mental health begins before we're born? As soon as our brains start developing, there are things that contribute to our mental health. There are also many factors to consider when mental illness becomes part of the conversation. Don't worry, we'll get to all of this in a few pages!

It can be hard to talk about mental health. But, without open discussion, kids can get the idea that mental health and mental illness are embarrassing, scary, or shameful. And, they might not feel safe or comfortable going to their grownups when they have questions or concerns of their own.

Open conversations can help kids build a strong foundation for positive mental health from an early age. Then, when they run into times of mental health struggles or mental illness, they will be equipped with the words and skills they need.

Together, we can help everyone (kids and grownups!) feel empowered to talk about mental health and mental illness in a safe, respectful, and joyful way.

Have you ever heard the term

"mental

How about

"mental

health"?
illness"?

Maybe you've heard them before because LOTS more people talk about mental health and mental illness today than they used to. Which is great!

But perhaps this is something new for you!

Mental health

describes how we're doing.

It includes

our experiences,

our thoughts,

our feelings,

our behaviors,

and our interactions
with other people.

Sometimes, we can tell how someone is doing by looking at behaviors that we can see. (Like if their voice is loud or quiet, whether their face looks happy or sad, or how calm their body is.)

But sometimes we only know how someone is doing based on what they tell us.

(We can't read each other's minds!)

Often, conversations about mental health begin when there are concerns or something feels wrong.

But mental health is ALWAYS there, and can be positive or negative regardless of whether a person has a diagnosable condition.

Mental health is made up of many things, and it's way more than just the opposite of being sick.

So, what contributes to our mental health?

Well, a lot of things!

But for starters...

genetics (characteristics you get from your biological parents),

relationships,

physical health,

the experiences we have,

community,

and government policies

are all some of the ingredients that make up mental health.

Everyone experiences some times when our mental health is at its best and times when it is not as good.

Perhaps it was a time when you felt happy, proud, excited about life, connected with other people, or were able to adapt to changes around you.

When our thoughts, feelings, behaviors, or interactions become difficult to manage, that may suggest we are struggling with our mental health. (Which again, is not the same as mental illness!)

Can you think of a time when your mental health was *not* at its best?

Maybe this was a time when you felt sad, overwhelmed, upset, or disconnected from other people.

Maybe something difficult happened in your life and you weren't sure how to get through it, or you didn't have the support you needed.

And mental health challenges look different for each person, even within your own family!

Some people behave in hurtful ways or use mean words.

Some people feel their worries on the inside but don't show it.

Some people have difficulty managing relationships with family or friends.

Some people have difficulty getting through daily activities like school or work successfully.

Mental health challenges are a completely normal, human experience!

But sometimes, if the difficulty goes on for a long time or makes it hard to do the things we need to do each day, we give it a name—either a broad one like "mental illness," or a specific medical diagnosis.

A diagnosis helps the right people provide the kind of support needed to help you feel and function better.

As we get older, our diagnosis may stay the same, or it might change. (A diagnosis isn't always permanent.)

Mental illness needs to be
diagnosed by a professional.

When we go to the doctor for the physical health of our bodies—like a broken bone or an ear infection—they can help us understand what's going on, what they can do to help, and what we can do to heal.

Our mental health works the same way as our physical health!

(But no shots! A mental health professional's tools are books, toys, talking, and in some cases, medicine prescribed to help you!!)

Whether we have a diagnosed mental illness or not, if life feels hard, there are things we can do and people who can help support our best mental health.

First of all,

KNOW YOU'RE NOT ALONE.

There is nothing shameful about needing help with your mental health.

Sometimes, our thoughts can be difficult to talk about. Or, they can become scary and make us feel stuck in our fear, anger, or worry.

Telling a trusted grownup how you're feeling is a great first step.

AND I want you to know something: the more we talk about hard things, the less scary those things become.

SERIO

OUSLY!

Here are some words that can help:

"I feel mad (or sad, or worried) and I don't know why."

"Sometimes, it feels hard to control my body."

"My stomach hurts a lot of the time."

"I feel like my brain is always moving and it won't slow down."

"Sometimes, my brain tells me to do things I know I shouldn't."

"My friends don't want to play with me and I don't know what to do."

Does any of that sound familiar?

Can you think of anything else?

If you want, take a moment to talk with your grownup about what you're thinking.

When you're ready to keep going, turn the page (but, no rush).

We usually can't change *everything* about the challenging situations we face, but we can learn new skills to help us respond to them.

Taking deep breaths, counting to 10, or taking a break outside can help us start to feel better and improve our mental health.*

*These are only some of the things grownups and professionals can teach you to help you manage your mental health—there are lots more too!

So, what questions do you have about mental health?

THE MORE WE ASK, THE MORE WE LEARN.

Approaching our mental health with curiosity, openness, and empathy can help us talk about it in our families, with our friends, and in our schools and communities.

What is something you can say or do today to care for your mental health?

(Your grownups can help you think it through!)

Got it?

OK...now, try it out!

And one more thing,

KEEP PRIORITIZING YOUR MENTAL HEALTH EVERY DAY!

Resources

Here are a few resources to keep the conversation going with the kids in your life!

A Kids Book About Anxiety
A Kids Book About Depression
A Kids Book About Trauma
A Kids Book About Therapy

University of Minnesota Extension Resources:
extension.umn.edu/mental-wellbeing/
mental-health#for-educators-3409511

extension.umn.edu/mental-wellbeing/
early-childhood-mental-health-toolkit

sites.google.com/umn.edu/
mentalflourishingtoolkit/home

Minnesota Association for Children's Mental Health (MACMH):
macmh.org

Minnesota Association for Children's Mental Health, Infant and Early Childhood (MAMCH-IEC):
macmh.org/infant-and-early-childhood